THE SCENTED LAVENDER BOOK

by

Lois Vickers

NORFOLK LAVENDER LTD

*N*orfolk Lavender Ltd was founded in 1932 and is England's last full-scale lavender farm, so we feel it is quite fair to describe ourselves as the home of English Lavender. English lavender oil and lavender flowers have long been highly-prized and known worldwide.

Every year we welcome to the farm over 100,000 visitors. They are fascinated to see the diversity within the National Collection of Lavenders, the process of distillation, and the fields of lavender during harvest-time. If all the plants in Norfolk Lavender's 100 acres (40 hectares) were laid end to end they would stretch for 120 miles (192 kilometres).

If you are not already a devotee of lavender, I am sure this book will convince you of the many charms and astonishing versatility of the plant, making you keen to experiment with its uses and eager to grow many of the more unusual lavenders mentioned in these pages. It could be the start of a life-long interest.

Henry Head

Norfolk Lavender Ltd
Caley Mill
Heacham
King's Lynn
Norfolk
PE31 7JE

Box 602
Dawsonville
Georgia 30534
USA

THE SCENTED LAVENDER BOOK

by

Lois Vickers

A BULFINCH PRESS BOOK
LITTLE, BROWN AND COMPANY
BOSTON   TORONTO   LONDON

For my father, Donovan Russell Vickers

First North American Edition

ISBN 0–8212–1836–0
Library of Congress Catalog Card Number 91–70011
Library of Congress Cataloging-in-Publication information is available.
Bulfinch Press is an imprint and trademark of Little, Brown and Company (Inc.)
Published simultaneously in Canada by Little, Brown & Company (Canada) Limited

PRINTED IN GREAT BRITAIN

Like all herbs, lavender can be dangerous if misused. To the best of the author's knowledge
the recommendations given will cause no harm but care must always be taken and
advice should be sought from medical and herbal authorities for medical conditions.

IMPORTANT NOTE: All recipe measurements give the Imperial amount first,
followed by the metric and then the U.S. equivalent. As these are not exact equivalents,
please work from one set of figures. U.S. teaspoons, tablespoons, pints, quarts and
gallons are all smaller than Imperial ones.

CONTENTS

INTRODUCTION	6
THE PLANT WITH A PAST	8
COOKING WITH LAVENDER	13
THE GARDENERS' FAVOURITE	22
DECORATIVE LAVENDER	36
LAVENDER AND LINEN	52
THE ESSENTIAL OIL	62
BIBLIOGRAPHY	79
INDEX	80

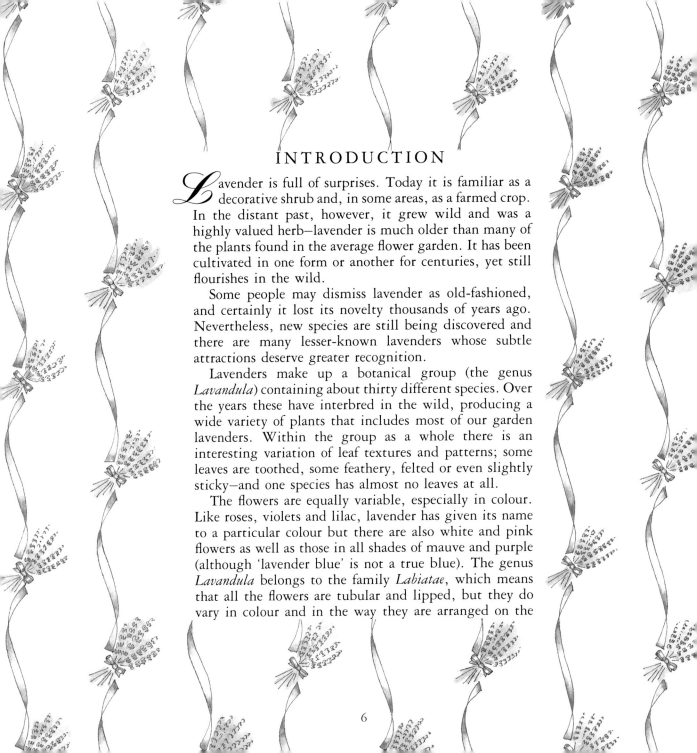

INTRODUCTION

*L*avender is full of surprises. Today it is familiar as a decorative shrub and, in some areas, as a farmed crop. In the distant past, however, it grew wild and was a highly valued herb—lavender is much older than many of the plants found in the average flower garden. It has been cultivated in one form or another for centuries, yet still flourishes in the wild.

Some people may dismiss lavender as old-fashioned, and certainly it lost its novelty thousands of years ago. Nevertheless, new species are still being discovered and there are many lesser-known lavenders whose subtle attractions deserve greater recognition.

Lavenders make up a botanical group (the genus *Lavandula*) containing about thirty different species. Over the years these have interbred in the wild, producing a wide variety of plants that includes most of our garden lavenders. Within the group as a whole there is an interesting variation of leaf textures and patterns; some leaves are toothed, some feathery, felted or even slightly sticky—and one species has almost no leaves at all.

The flowers are equally variable, especially in colour. Like roses, violets and lilac, lavender has given its name to a particular colour but there are also white and pink flowers as well as those in all shades of mauve and purple (although 'lavender blue' is not a true blue). The genus *Lavandula* belongs to the family *Labiatae*, which means that all the flowers are tubular and lipped, but they do vary in colour and in the way they are arranged on the flowering heads. Some flower heads are shaped like ears of corn, but others are like tiny pine cones, are three-pronged or have delicate or flamboyant bracts.

Oil from lavender flowers has been used for several hundred years in the perfume industry, but it has other functions that are much older. Its medicinal properties are ancient history yet today they are being discovered anew by aromatherapists. Lavender oil has always been invaluable in health care and for domestic tasks, and the flowers and leaves can also add a mysterious piquancy to both savoury and sweet dishes.

THE CHARM OF LAVENDER

The scent of lavender is a major part of its attraction, and one reason why it is a favourite shrub of gardeners past and present. Another reason must be its versatility: lavenders range in size from large and stately plants to charming miniature forms, and they can make hedges, join in mixed plantings or stand out as specimen shrubs or groups.

Indoors, lavender also has many decorative uses. Lavender and linens have a long-standing affinity and embroiderers will find lavenders rewarding to grow and inspiring to use. They will be continuing a long tradition: there are countless references to lavender in old books and manuscripts, recipes, household hints and gardening tips. Some of these are rather whimsical but most are practical, being useful and gentle alternatives to harsh modern approaches. No other garden shrub can match lavender's unique blend of appealing characteristics.

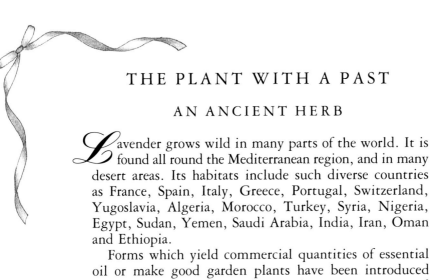

THE PLANT WITH A PAST

AN ANCIENT HERB

*L*avender grows wild in many parts of the world. It is found all round the Mediterranean region, and in many desert areas. Its habitats include such diverse countries as France, Spain, Italy, Greece, Portugal, Switzerland, Yugoslavia, Algeria, Morocco, Turkey, Syria, Nigeria, Egypt, Sudan, Yemen, Saudi Arabia, India, Iran, Oman and Ethiopia.

Forms which yield commercial quantities of essential oil or make good garden plants have been introduced into countries where they would not have occurred naturally. Among the places where lavenders are cultivated are France, Japan, the Netherlands, Belgium, Germany, Bulgaria, the USA, the USSR, Australia, Canada, Romania and Britain. It is truly a universal plant!

It is difficult to be precise about the origins of lavender because the earliest reports may be misleading. Botanical and etymological confusion were sometimes made worse by mistakes in translation. However, the Greek writer Dioscorides, who compiled a list of plants and their

Lavandula stoechas

medicinal uses which remained authoritative until the sixteenth century, is reliable. Writing in the first century AD, he made it clear that the first lavender to be known widely and used medicinally was *Lavandula stoechas*, although it was not until much later that it was recognized as a member of the lavender family.

L. canariensis

L. stoechas has been a garden favourite for centuries. It thrives in pots, which can be moved under cover if bad weather threatens.

One early practical use for aromatic plants, including lavender, was strewing. The lack of personal hygiene in previous centuries must have had literally breathtaking effects at times, so strong-smelling herbs were frequently scattered over floors to disguise unpleasant odours and act as a combined deodorant, antiseptic and insecticide. Precious cultivated herbs are unlikely to have been used but, instead, peasants would have gathered other suitable plants. *L. stoechas* was a very likely choice, because it grows profusely in the wild and its foliage is strongly balsamic, especially when trampled upon.

L. multifida

According to Dioscorides, *L. stoechas* was 'good for ye griefs in ye thorax'. Water and flower heads were boiled to a decoction.

Strewing lavender on the floor is hardly practical these days but there is an attractive variation on the theme. When laying a new carpet, I like to sprinkle a thin layer of dried lavender flowers on the floor or between the underlay and carpet. Periodically I top that up with a light sprinkling of pure lavender oil which evaporates quickly, leaving behind a sweeter scent than any artificial air freshener.

LAVENDER SPECIES

L. stoechas belongs to a group of lavenders that are recognizable by the distinctive coloured bracts decorating the flower heads, making them desirable garden or

L. pinnata

conservatory plants. The other plants in the group are *L. dentata*, which has indented leaves, and *L. viridis*, which is the greenest lavender. *L. stoechas* was very useful as a medicinal plant, and is still reported to be used in Islamic medicine, but was superseded by *L. latifolia* and *L. angustifolia* (especially the latter) when it was realised that they give good yields of oil and have therapeutic qualities. These had another advantage in being good garden plants, whereas most of the other known lavenders could only be used decoratively or in herbal infusions, because their oils were not plentiful or useful enough.

Among the other decorative lavenders which had been written about by 1817 are *L. canariensis, L. multifida* and *L. pinnata,* which all have more or less lacy leaves. All three are known to gardeners in Europe, Australia and the USA, but they belong to a much larger group of about fifteen species altogether, most of which have not been much brought into cultivation as yet. A later find, *L. lanata,* was not reported by botanists until 1837. Its thickly felted silvery foliage makes it very much a garden plant, and botanically it belongs with *L. angustifolia* and *L. latifolia*.

There are two other botanical sub-groups, which between them contain ten more species, all of which fall outside the scope of this book because they grow in India, Somalia, Socotra and the Arabian peninsula.

It is lavender's adaptability which has made it so widespread and well-loved. It grows naturally in dry, rocky or sandy places, but some lavenders adapt readily to less extreme conditions. Cuttings and seeds are both good travellers, and so have contributed to the distribution of

2065 LA COTE D'AZUR — La Cueillette de la Lavande.

Carshalton Lavender Fields. Bunching Lavender for Market.

Above: Harvesting French lavender on the Côte d'Azur.
Below: Bunching English lavender for market.

11

lavender around the world, and early travellers would have carried it for its therapeutic properties.

LAVENDER OIL

Over the centuries, oils from *L. angustifolia* and *L. latifolia* have served a huge variety of purposes, including domestic, medical, industrial and cosmetic ones. For example, lavender oil is a traditional ingredient of good-quality polishes for wooden furniture and floors.

The best lavender oil (from *L. angustifolia*) is rather too expensive to be tipped liberally into a tin of polish. Its cheaper alternative, spike oil (from *L. latifolia*), can be bought from many chemists. Try adding 2½ teaspoons (12 ml) of each of the two oils to your favourite furniture cream, or to wax polish warmed first (in its tin) in a *bain-marie*. You could also use the third sort of lavender oil, lavandin oil, which comes from a hybrid plant. 'Lavandin' is the French name given to hybrids between *L. angustifolia* and *L. latifolia*, and both the plant and its oil have some of the attributes of both parents.

Lavender hybrids usually arise through cross-fertilization by insects, but mainly bees. There is a long list of lavender hybrids and another of lavender cultivars. A hybrid is a cross between two different species or varieties of the same genus (in this case, the genus *Lavandula*). Variants of typical plant forms are called 'varieties' if they occur in the wild and 'cultivars' if they occur in cultivation. Their differences can be perpetuated by propagation.

Lavender of any sort has always been important to beekeepers because, as well as containing oil, the flowers provide nectar. Lavender honey is delicious, and distinctive. Bees prefer lavender to anything else that may be in flower at the same time, so if the hives are near a lavender plantation the bees have no need to search elsewhere for food.

COOKING WITH LAVENDER

*W*e cook with all sorts of herbs and spices, so why does it seem strange to cook with lavender? Perhaps it is because lavender is almost exclusively associated with perfume, yet rosemary, which has also been used in perfumery for hundreds of years, is fully accepted as a culinary herb. Try cooking with lavender—its leaves are good if used sparingly in savoury dishes, especially with cheese, and also give an unusual flavour to roast lamb or chicken. Lavender flower spikes and leaves can be steeped in oil or vinegar for salad dressings, or included in herb mixtures. Lavender also blends well with tangy or slightly bitter flavours, and particularly with citrus fruits; a sprinkling of flowers will transform half a grapefruit into a special dish.

For sweet mixtures, it is often best to use the flowers for flavouring and then discard them. Tie them in a muslin bag when making an infusion or sieve them out of thicker mixtures once their flavour has been absorbed (usually overnight). Fresh lavender looks lovely decorating a serving platter or garnishing food, but don't scatter whole flower heads over puddings—their taste is too strong and the texture too fibrous.

Using flowers in food, both decoratively and as a flavouring, is a very old custom, and in the past the flowers would have been eaten with all the more pleasure because they looked so pretty. Such treats were often served at special feasts, and that is a tradition worth continuing. Somehow it is easier to try something out of the ordinary at a celebration buffet, where you are free to help yourself and where there are alternatives if you do not enjoy what you have chosen. Floral food can be out of place at an ordinary dinner party.

Even so, there is a very pretty way to use the whole flowers which should not frighten anybody. The suitable flowers come from *Lavandula angustifolia* (for example, 'Hidcote' or 'Munstead'), or from hybrids between *L. angustifolia* and *L. latifolia* (such as 'Seal', 'Grappenhall' or 'Grosso'). Other lavenders may have flowers which are too small or lack the true lavender scent. Pick plenty of dry flower heads and, having selected perfect flowers, pull the corolla (the funnel of petals) from the calyx (the enclosing bud) of each flower, until you have enough. They will look and taste delightful scattered across a creamy lavender custard (made with lavenderized sugar).

Flower head or spike—consists of lots of separate flowers. Use only for decoration or infusion.

CRYSTALLIZED LAVENDER FLOWERS

If you have the patience and dexterity for which cake decorators are renowned, you can crystallize lavender flowers to make the most delicate cake decorations. My first attempts resulted only in inelegant, inedible, crunchy blobs, because I was using the whole flower spike—try single flowers instead. Choose plenty of the biggest blooms with the strongest colouring (paler flowers are less effective). Pull out the corollas and spread them over a tea towel.

Whisk one egg white in its own volume of water. Skim off the froth and paint the inside and outside of each petal with the liquid; you must paint them thoroughly without

One whole flower or floret—use sparingly in salads.

Detach and use corolla (petals) alone in sweet dishes, remove calyx and discard.

drenching them. You will probably have to handle the flowers with tweezers, picking them up by the narrow white end of the corolla. Coat them with sifted icing sugar, shake off any excess and transfer them to a baking tray covered with non-stick parchment.

Bake them for at least two hours, in the bottom of the coolest possible oven, until they are completely dry and crisp. They look marvellous decorating a plain white-iced cake. The crystallized flowers are very delicate, so handle them with care and, if you must store them, spread them in a single layer in an airtight container.

LAVENDER IN SALADS

Today's salads often contain a colourful blend of edible flowers, and lavender can be part of that mix or used by itself—it combines well with bitter leaves. Fresh lavender flowers look much prettier than dried ones (which should be used very sparingly), but in both cases you should use individual flowers and not whole flower heads. The flowers can be mixed with nasturtiums, marigold petals, borage flowers or other petals, but I think they look spectacular on their own.

For a simple salad, cut about forty heads of lavender (the darker the flowers, the better). Detach the individual flowers from their spikes by grasping the petals gently and pulling slowly. Arrange a selection of pale chicory leaves on a platter together with thin slices of avocado brushed with lemon juice. Drizzle them with a lemony dressing, then sprinkle with the lavender flowers.

LAVENDER MARMALADE

This recipe comes from Norfolk Lavender Ltd in England.
For a less sweet marmalade, reduce the sugar.

2¼ lb (1 kg/2¼ lb) Seville oranges, scrubbed
1 lemon, scrubbed
3½ pints (2 litres/8½ cups) water
4½ lb (2 kg/9 cups) preserving (granulated) sugar
1½ oz (35 g/1½ oz) dried lavender flowers,
tied in a muslin bag

Cut the fruit in half, extract the juice and keep to one side, and place the pips in a muslin bag. You can shred the peel if you wish, and remove some of the pith if it is very thick. Place the peel, juice and water in a large pan, add the muslin bag of pips and bring to the boil. Simmer gently for 1½ hours, stirring occasionally, until the peel is tender. Squeeze the bag of pips to release any liquid and discard. Warm the sugar by placing it in a large bowl in a cool oven, then stir it into the liquid over a gentle heat until it has dissolved. Add the muslin bag of lavender and fast boil the mixture for 10 minutes. Press the juice from the bag and discard. Continue to fast boil the mixture until setting point is reached. (If using a thermometer, setting point is 221°F [105°C]. If not, spoon a little marmalade on to a chilled saucer, cool and then push your finger across its surface—it will wrinkle when it has reached setting point.) Leave to cool for ½ hour, stir well and then ladle into cleaned, warmed and dry jars.

The hint of lavender is discernible but not overpowering and it really does improve the marmalade. To save time, you can do as the Norfolk Lavender cooks do to keep up with demand: use canned, prepared citrus fruit (but only the sort with no added preservatives).

LAVENDER YOGHURT ICE

This dessert captures the essence of summery days.
It makes 1½ pints (0.9 litres/3¾ cups).

¼ pint (150 ml/⅔ cup) gin
½ pint (300 ml/1⅓ cups) plain yoghurt
9 fl oz (250 ml/1 cup) water
juice of one lemon
1 banana, sliced (not too big nor too ripe)
2 egg whites
7 oz (175 g/⅞ cup) sugar
scant 3 tbsp (45 ml/3 tbsp) fresh lavender flowers

Place the gin, sugar, water and flowers in a large pan and
heat gently, stirring until the sugar has dissolved and the
mixture is just coming to the boil. Immediately remove
from the heat and cover. Leave to infuse for 10 minutes.
Meanwhile, liquidize the sliced banana with the lemon
juice. Strain the gin infusion and leave to cool, then add
it to the banana and liquidize again. Whip the egg whites
and fold them into the mixture. Pour into a metal freezer
tray and place in the freezer, but take it out every 30
minutes and stir well. The egg whites will tend to separate
and give a frothy top but if you continue to stir them in
they will eventually coagulate. While the mixture is still
mushy, stir in the yoghurt and freeze until firm, but
continue to stir every 30 minutes to get a good texture.
The result should be pale pink and scented, with a smooth
light consistency.

LAVENDER MERINGUES

These would be ideal for a special occasion. Makes about 30 meringue shells.

9 oz (250 g/2 ¼ cups) icing sugar
half a lemon
whites of 4 medium eggs
3 tbsp (45 ml/3 tbsp) dried lavender flowers
3 tbsp (45 ml/3 tbsp) granulated sugar

Place the lavender flowers and granulated sugar in an electric coffee grinder and pulverize until you get a very fine dust. Sift with the icing sugar into a bowl. Tip the egg whites into a clean bowl, add a drop of lemon juice and whisk until stiff. Using a metal spoon, carefully fold in the lavender and sugar. Cover a baking tray with non-stick baking parchment and place small dollops of the mixture on the tray, ensuring each one is at least 1 inch (2.5 cm) away from its neighbours. Place in a preheated oven, set at 225°F (110°C), Gas Mark ¼, for about three hours until risen and crisp, but still pale duck egg blue. Switch off the oven. Scoop out any soggy pieces of meringue then replace in the oven to dry out fully.

Sandwich together with lavender cream. To make this, mix 9 fl oz (250 ml/1 cup) double (heavy) cream with 2 tbsp (30 ml/2 tbsp) fresh or 1 tbsp (15 ml/1 tbsp) dried lavender flowers. Refrigerate overnight then strain the cream and discard flowers. Beat until fairly stiff, then gradually add 1 tbsp (15 ml/1 tbsp) sifted icing sugar, beating continuously until stiff.

PERFUMED SUGAR

It is worth experimenting with lavender in sweet recipes, where its pungency is unusual and refreshing. Sugar perfumed with lavender is a traditional confection, and makes original sauces and desserts. To make it, bruise about 20 dried flower heads and store in an airtight container with 1 lb (450 g/2 cups) sugar. If you perfume icing sugar in this way, the lavender helps to make glacé icing less sweet and sickly.

SYRUPS AND LIQUEURS

Lavender syrups and liqueurs are excellent for relieving the symptoms of colds. The syrup can be diluted with hot water and brandy in the winter, or carbonated mineral water in the summer. Put 8 oz (225 g/8 oz) dried lavender flowers (off the stalk) into a pan then pour on 32 fl oz (900 ml/4 cups) boiling water and mash them gently with a wooden spoon as they start to swell. Add 1 lb (450 g/ 2 cups) sugar and stir until dissolved, then simmer for 5 minutes. Leave to infuse for about an hour, then sieve the mixture and pass it through a coffee filter paper. You can simmer it again to thicken the syrup but you will lose some of the volatile oils. Pour into a sterilized bottle and store in the refrigerator.

You can make a liqueur with an unusual tang by warming 16 fl oz (450 ml/2 cups) vodka or gin and stirring in 1 lb (450 g/2 cups) sugar and 8 oz (225 g/8 oz) fresh lavender flowers. Add a handful of dried lemon verbena leaves (*Aloysia triphylla*) or lemon balm (*Melissa officinalis*).

Stir well, cover the pan and leave overnight to infuse. Strain and filter the liqueur in the same way as for the syrup, then pour into a sterilized bottle and leave for up to three months in a cool dark place before drinking. If you can't spare so many lavender flowers, use what you do have and leave the bottled liqueur for longer before drinking.

LAVENDER TEA

Many Europeans drink lavender tea to soothe their nerves, although it is less common in the UK and USA. Lavenders vary, and so do tastes, so start by using 1 tsp (5 ml/1 tsp) dried lavender flowers to every 8 fl oz (225 ml/1 cup) boiling water. Make it in a pot just as you would ordinary tea and leave to brew for a few minutes, then add more water if necessary and sweeten with honey.

An infusion, or tisane, of lavender is a proven remedy for nervous tension and headaches. It is a good reviver!

Lavender sugar is an idea that comes from 17th-century England. You can use fresh flowers instead of dried but you will need double the amount.

Use lavender to make an interesting liqueur with a very pretty colour.

As well as diluting lavender syrup for drinks, you can pour it over ice cream or use it as a flavouring.

THE GARDENERS' FAVOURITE

LAVENDER SPECIES

*T*his illustration shows both how decorative and different lavender leaves can be. The outer border shows leaves of *Lavandula dentata*. As its name suggests, the leaves are toothed, or cut, very finely and regularly. Under the influence of different conditions, the leaf shape becomes stretched or compressed lengthways, opening or closing the indentations and giving the plant a fern-like appearance. The leaves are a bright, fresh green. The cultivar *L. dentata candicans* has pale, heavily-felted leaves.

The border inside this is of the leaves of *L. angustifolia* 'Nana Alba', which are small and fine. The whole plant has the delicate appeal of the miniature, and is also known as 'dwarf white' or affectionately as 'baby white'. There are several other white-flowered lavenders available, but you will know this particular one because of its charm and small size.

The eight large, finely-cut leaves are of *L. multifida*, an uncharacteristic lavender which in many locations behaves like an annual, even when not attacked by frost, despite being a perennial. It sprawls but is not untidy.

The four central leaves are of *L. lanata*, which means 'woolly'. This term perfectly describes them for they look as though they could have been cut from felt. Their pale, soft grey lasts well when they are dried and they look pretty in pot-pourri. Felting is a natural protection against drought and indicates that the plant is not equipped to survive if there is the slightest hint of waterlogging.

NAMING NAMES

*W*e all think we know lavender, but do we? Although we know it was introduced into gardens centuries ago from the wild, and is one of the best-known and most loved of all cultivated plants, some aspects of lavender's past are muddled and mysterious, and some of the names it has been given have caused confusion.

Gardeners usually like to have some information about the plants they grow. At the very least, knowing the correct name and original habitat of a plant will tell the gardener whether he or she can provide it with the right conditions in which it will flourish. That is particularly important for shrubs such as lavender, which are not as short-term as bedding plants. Anyone who gardens on soggy acid soil, sticky clay or in a shady site may have failed with lavender through being unaware of its origins in the French Alps. This may be caused by the familiar label 'Old English lavender', which is misleading because lavender is not an English plant at all. It is ironic that of all countries where lavender has been cultivated, England has been so fervent in taking lavender to its heart. English lavender is known worldwide, yet there is really no such thing in botanical terms—just lavender which is cultivated in England. There has never been a native English species and there is no wild lavender in England.

LAVENDER IN MITCHAM

Mitcham, a borough near London, gave its name to more lavender than was actually grown there, and at one time

Potter and Moore, another old English company, used this label for many years and it acquired more than a touch of romantic nostalgia. In Spain, however, spike lavender was transported to stills by donkey until well into the 1970s.

the name 'Mitcham lavender' had as much force as 'Scotch whisky' or 'Ceylon tea' as an assurance of good quality. So successful were the English growers in associating lavender water with Mitcham that it became almost like a brand name, and its renown lingers even today, although the Mitcham distilleries have long since disappeared.

Similarly, the phrase 'Old English lavender' has overtones of traditional worthiness, and was adopted by various English manufacturers, notably Yardley's, whose lavender toiletries were made in England but not necessarily from exclusively English oils. Indeed, English lavender has such a reputation for good quality that some manufacturers are happy to pass off their lavender water as being made with English oil when it is not. The only company producing a wide range of products in which the lavender oils are exclusively English is Norfolk Lavender. They thus have a genuine right to use the description 'English lavender'.

British settlers took lavender with them to Australia, where it grows well, on plantations as well as in gardens. The name 'Mitcham lavender' was exported too, but it seems to have become separated from the plant with which it emigrated. Mysteriously, the plant to which it is now attached, *Lavandula* x *allardii*, seems unlikely to have been grown in Mitcham in the first place. It is a hybrid which originated in cultivation, and both its parents (*L. latifolia* and *L. dentata*) are too delicate for British winters.

In any case, there is no single cultivar which could be called the definitive Mitcham lavender. Commercial growers were competing amongst themselves and with foreign growers, and their search for high oil yields is likely to have matched that of French growers, who started with true lavender (*L. angustifolia*) and later moved on to hybrids (lavandin).

French growers cultivated various selected forms of lavandin, all of which are large, vigorous plants with fragrant, densely packed flower spikes, like the ones grown in Mitcham, but without the indented leaves of *L.* x *allardii*. There is a cultivar of *L. angustifolia*, named 'Mitcham Grey', which may have been grown in Mitcham, but is no more the definitive Mitcham lavender than any other form.

OTHER MISLEADING NAMES

'Old English' and 'Dutch' are names given to two garden plants which may both have started life in France. They are straight-leaved hybrid lavenders (lavandin or *L.* x *intermedia*) which are often confused with each other, although 'Old English' is the larger of the two plants. They are both also sold as *L. spica*, a name which should not now be used. 'Dutch' is one of the most popular garden lavenders in the USA, UK and the Netherlands. Both have caused confusion as they have been taken to indicate the country where the plant occurs naturally, or have been applied to other, similar, cultivars. The other nationalistic names (French, Spanish and Italian) are virtually interchangeable, making them inaccurate and unhelpful; they should be disregarded.

'French Lavender' is the worst offender, because it is applied to more than one species of lavender and to

Lavandula angustifolia

'Imperial Gem'
'Princess Blue'
'Royal Purple'
'Hidcote'
'Nana Alba'
'Twickel Purple'
'Loddon Blue'
'Alba'
'Rosea'
'Munstead'
'Bowles Early'
'Nana Atropurpurea'
'Gray Lady'
'Mitcham Grey'
'Warburton Gem'
'Irene Doyle'
'Maillette'
'Gwendolyn Anley'
'Dwarf Blue'
'Backhouse Purple'
'Summerland Supreme'
'Compacta'
'Middachten'
'Graves'
'Folgate'
'Fragrance'

Lavandula x *intermedia*

'Super'
'Abrial'
'Sumian'
'Spécial Grégoire'
'Standard'
'Maime Epis Tête'
'Provence'

All these varieties have been used for commercial oil production, as has 'Grosso', which is now the most widely planted. It is laden with flowers and more colourful than any of the well-known garden lavandins (listed below) and is highly disease-resistant.

'Seal'
'Dutch'
'Grappenhall'
'Hidcote Giant'
'Alba'
'Grey Hedge'
'Waltham Giant'
'Old English'
'Silver Gray'

Santolina chamaecyparissus, whose common name is cotton lavender or lavender cotton. Santolina has no connection with lavender, nor with cotton, and belongs to a completely different botanical family from lavender, as does another impostor, sea lavender (*Limonium sinuatum*, sometimes called 'statice').

Botanists often chastise gardeners for using common names for plants instead of Latin ones, and the confusions within the lavender family lend weight to their complaints. Common names are often venerable and picturesque, and usually charming, but they are inherently parochial and subjective, and they do not help the spread of understanding.

However, botanists themselves are not blameless, although their mistakes can usually be traced. One of the worst cases of mistaken identity in the lavender family was perpetrated by one of the most influential botanists of all time. Linnaeus was a Swedish botanist who, in the eighteenth century, devised the first rational system for classifying plants and one which is still used today.

Linnaeus regarded two separate species of lavender (*L. angustifolia* and *L. latifolia*) as not separate but rather varieties of the same species, and named them accordingly as *L. spica*. Because his system of classification is so authoritative and widely respected, the mistake made by Linnaeus has been hard to correct. *L. spica* was eventually recognized as an ambiguous name and has been outlawed. Nurserymen in particular should be scrupulous in identifying the plants they sell, yet it is not uncommon to see a whole tray of one sort of lavender labelled as another.

IDENTIFYING DIFFERENT LAVENDERS

*R*ecognizing those lavenders which have cut leaves (*Lavandula pinnata, L. canariensis, L. multifida, L. dentata* etc) is easy because they are distinct from each other and also from plain-leaved lavenders. *L. stoechas, L. pedunculata* and *L. viridis* can be distinguished from other straight-leaved lavenders by the showy bracts which decorate and crown the flower heads. In the case of *L. pedunculata*, the bracts are very gaudy and can be as much as 2 in (5 cm) long. The greatest confusion arises between the lavenders which in the past were grouped together under Linnaeus' incorrect name, *L. spica* (see page 27).

GARDEN LAVENDERS

Linnaeus' classification has been updated, and according to the most recent botanical information, straight-leaved garden lavenders fall quite neatly into two groups (see page 26). One group is of *L. angustifolia* cultivars and the other is *L.* x *intermedia* (lavandin), a hybrid of *L. angustifolia* and *L. latifolia*. The latter is a large branching plant with wide leaves, which for many years has formed the basis of the Spanish spike oil industry. It can be hard to find in nurseries, and many plants sold under that name are in fact hybrids. It's easy to tell which plant you have (but only after you have bought it) because proper *L. latifolia* will multiply from seed whereas hybrids (lavandin) are nearly always sterile and must be propagated from cuttings.

KEY

Bracts:

a L. stoechas
b L. pedunculata
c L. dentata
d L. pyrenaica
e L. x *intermedia*
f L. latifolia

g calyces of various forms of L. angustifolia

Flowers:

h L. stoechas
i L. multifida

Leaves:

j L. x *allardii*
k L. viridis
l L. x *intermedia*
m L. latifolia
n L. angustifolia
o L. stoechas
p L. pinnata
q typical lavender seedling

L. latifolia flourishes in Mediterranean gardens but other than that it is rare, perhaps because it is not the most obviously gardenworthy lavender. Another reason is that, despite not being so demanding as *L. angustifolia* about its soil chemistry, it is more fussy about physical conditions, and readily succumbs to damp and frost.

CULTIVATION REQUIREMENTS

All lavenders must have very good drainage and a good circulation of fresh air if they are to be happy. Most prefer full sun, although some varieties of *L. angustifolia* (notably *L. delphinensis*) grow larger and prefer richer soil, colder weather and less sun. It is perhaps from this type that lavender species popular in the UK and the Netherlands were first selected. *L. angustifolia* prefers a chalky soil whereas hybrids (lavandins) have inherited from *L. latifolia* a tolerance of slightly acid soil and will not thrive in very chalky areas. Most lavenders do very well in sandy soil, pure sand or gravel, as these all imitate the conditions of their natural habitat in the Alps. Such gritty soils are especially useful in flat areas where drainage is a problem; it is vital that lavender roots are never waterlogged.

Commercial growers know that the quality and quantity of the oil produced by their plants is directly affected by the climate, with sun and more sun being the main requirement. This concerns amateur gardeners too, because in less than ideal conditions the flower spikes will be weak and overlong. The number of spikes will be reduced and they will neither smell so delicious nor look so bountiful.

best from cuttings	
easy from seed	
beware of frost	
straight or cut edged leaf	
yields oil	
trident-form flower head	
sachets and pot-pourri coloured bracts	
good in containers	
relative flower colours	
small/medium/large plant	
relative leaf colour and hair	
more or less aromatic	
beware of winter wet	
domed spiky sprawling habit	
flowering season	

A GARDENER'S GUIDE

L. x *allardii*												
L. *angustifolia* (e.g. 'Hidcote')												
L. *angustifolia* (e.g. 'Nana Alba')												
L. *canariensis*												
L. *dentata*												
L. *dentata candicans*												
L. x *intermedia* (e.g. 'Grosso')												
L. x *intermedia* (e.g. 'Grappenhall')												
L. *lanata*												
L. *latifolia*												
L. *multifida*												
L. *pinnata*												
L. *pedunculata*												
L. *stoechas*												
L. *viridis*												

FLOWER COLOUR

*T*n the wild, most labiates produce flowers in a range of shades from white through pink to mauve and blue, and so do lavenders. The pink and white forms have a lower survival rate, so they are less common.

Although *L. stoechas* 'Alba' and *L. angustifolia* 'Nana Alba' are enchanting plants, the pink and white forms are often considered to have little more than novelty value. However they really come into their own at twilight. The pale flowers scent the evening air and they are more visible in poor light than darker blooms.

WHITE LAVENDERS

Five forms are generally available. The two smallest are both forms of *Lavandula angustifolia*—the tiny 'Nana Alba' and the medium 'Alba'. The white form of *L. stoechas* has flower heads with white bracts and grows well in a pot but it may need protection in the winter. *L. viridis* has greenish-white flower heads and bright green sticky leaves, and it can grow quite large. Again, it may need winter protection. A more robust, large plant is the white-flowered lavandin, *L.* x *intermedia* 'Alba'.

PINK LAVENDERS

With the exception of spontaneously occurring colour variations, all pink-flowered lavenders may be classified as forms of *L. angustifolia* 'Rosea'. With pink forms in particular, aim to buy plants when established and in flower, as the shades vary.

Lavenders are variable, and the same plant grown in different conditions or in different countries will produce a differently proportioned flower head. The illustration opposite indicates the relative sizes and characteristics of some lavenders. The largest, L. x allardii, may have a flower head six times larger than the smallest, L. angustifolia 'Nana Alba'.

L. x *allardii*
Lavandula dentata has hybridized with Lavandula latifolia and with Lavandula angustifolia to produce two similar plants, L. x allardii and L. x heterophylla. They are the largest of the lavenders and though less familiar in Europe they are more common in Australia and South Africa. The flower spikes are very large with many tightly packed flowers, and are characteristically curved and tapered at the top. ▷

L. *'Grosso'*
L. 'Grosso' has very fat flower heads crammed with flowers. Its name is not descriptive but refers to the man who first selected the plant, M. Pierre Grosso. ▷

L. *'Grappenhall'*
L. 'Grappenhall' is a traditional English garden lavender with a distinctively pea-green tinge to its foliage. ▷

L. latifolia has a flower spike which appears as greenish grey until the flowers bloom. They are less conspicuous than in garden lavenders. ▷

L. rosea – whorls of pink flowers are well separated. ▷
L. 'Hidcote' – a well-known lavender with the deepest purple calcyes. ▷

L. *Nana Alba* ▷

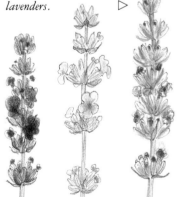

WAYS WITH LAVENDER

*I*n traditional gardens lavender looks wonderful grown as hedges or mixed with other shrubs and perennials. In cottage gardens, it is often too cramped and may become very leggy with few flowers. In the wild, lavenders are not particularly long-lived and they should not be relied upon as part of the permanent plantings in the garden. Although their lives can be prolonged by a good environment and regular severe pruning, they will usually be past their best after seven or eight years.

PROPAGATING LAVENDER PLANTS

As a rule, lavandin plants (*Lavandula* x *intermedia*) are propagated by cuttings, which root easily in a gritty compost. The cut-leaved species and those with tufts of showy bracts (*L. pinnata, L. multifida, L. dentata, L. stoechas,* etc) all set seed and will self-sow, as will *L. lanata*. They can also be propagated by cuttings, but rooting can be slow and sowing from seeds may be easier.

L. angustifolia can be grown by either method, but seeds will usually produce a variable crop of offspring. If you want to plant a dwarf hedge (Hidcote is ideal) you may save time and money by growing the plants from seed, but the results will not be uniform. The best method, time permitting, is to choose your ideal mature stock plant and then use the whole bush to take as many cuttings as you require. If you need so many plants that you would rather order them from a nursery, do ask for an undertaking that all the plants will be exact clones

Lavenders look marvellous in terracotta pots, preferably old or hand-made ones. The felted grey-green foliage of Lavandula lanata can be shown off to advantage in old weathered galvanized containers.

If you live in an area prone to cold winters you can grow lavenders in pots and move them under cover at the first sign of frost.

As lavenders have such strong connections with washday (as well as being used when rinsing clothes, they may have been a component of the wood-ash mixtures which preceded soaps and detergents) it seems appropriate to plant them in one of the old galvanized tubs that were once used to wash linens.

and not raised from seed, otherwise your hedge will be a hotchpotch of different plants.

PLANTS FOR GROUND COVER

Lavenders make good ground cover, especially on sloping, parched sites. *L. stoechas*, *L. pedunculata* and *L. dentata* are the best plants to choose as they will happily sprawl. Try to avoid using *L. angustifolia*, *L. latifolia* or their hybrids as they resent overcrowding (although they look good when well-spaced on a terraced site).

OTHER GARDENING IDEAS

Because they are so decorative, lavenders have countless uses in the garden. Try emphasizing their pale grey-green colours and soft textures by placing them with similar plants. *L. lanata* (which needs shelter from frost) looks good with the tiny leaves of *Raoulia hookeri*, or *R. australis*, and *Tanacetum haradjanii*, and they all enjoy good drainage and plenty of sun.

L. dentata candicans is a beautiful plant in its own right, though still uncommon in some countries. Its felted leaves go well with those of *Santolina chamaecyparissus*—the yellow buttons of santolina and the soft bluish lavender spikes are set off perfectly by the downy grey foliage.

Some lavenders tend to become leggy quite quickly, with *L. viridis* being a prime example. You could train it as a standard by pinching out the side shoots on the main stem of a suitably lanky softwood cutting until it has reached the height you wish, then pinching out the growing tip to give a bushy crown.

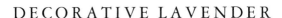

DECORATIVE LAVENDER

DRYING LAVENDER

*A*mong the flowers used for dried arrangements, lavender has much to recommend it. For instance, it dries easily, needing nothing but a good circulation of air, and keeps its colour for some time. Its stems stay strong and don't need wiring, unlike many other dried flowers. It looks good and smells lovely, and once dried it ages with the gentle charm of fading velveteen. An arrangement of fresh lavender flowers and foliage can be left to dry, or you can dry the lavender first and then arrange it—it's much less fragile than most dried flowers.

Dried arrangements often look rather aimless but lavender has a purposeful air. That is probably because the origin of the traditional bunch of lavender is a practical one—it was hung up to dry so the florets could be stripped off to make pot-pourri and sachets.

Lavender lasts well, although of course the scent may fade with time, and each summer brings a new harvest. Unlike so many modern pot-pourri mixtures, lavender has a clean and honest fragrance and can be revitalized with real essential lavender oil. Accept no substitute!

HOW TO DRY LAVENDER

Secure your bunches of lavender with strong elastic bands —the stems will shrink while drying and might slip through string—then hang them in a dry shady place. A roof space is ideal. Strong light will fade the flowers but

Dried lavender flowers are really just dried calyces. Some plants have green calyces, some various shades of purple and some are green suffused with purple. Only dark purple calyces keep a good colour when dried. The colours of hybrid lavenders soon fade but they are fine for short-term decorations.

When harvesting lavender for drying on the stem, pick it before the flowers are fully open otherwise they will drop during the drying process. If you are interested in pot-pourri or making sachets, and the fragrance is more important than the colour, then cut the lavender as late as you dare, but put newspaper underneath the branches to catch the dropping florets.

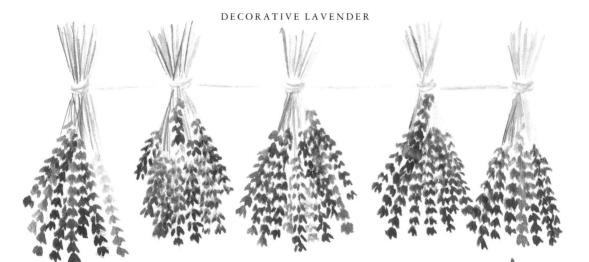

if you can only hang them in a sunny room you should first place them in brown paper bags for protection.

You can tie the bunches with ribbon or tape and use them for decoration just as they are, or arrange a mass of stalks in a suitable container. Cultivars of *Lavandula angustifolia* are a good choice because the flowers cling to the stalks when dried. If you use hybrid lavender (*L.* x *intermedia* or *lavandin*) for arrangements, you should handle the dried blooms with care because they are more easily dislodged from the stems. However, if you are stripping off the flowers, hybrid lavender is ideal.

Thoughts of drying lavender conjure up romantic scenes, like the one of Vita Sackville-West and her family on the sunny terrace at Long Barn, stripping lavender flowers from their stalks. It may be best to strip dried lavender outside because it can produce more dust than is comfortable. Some people enjoy lavender's sneeze-producing powers (it is an ingredient of some snuff mixtures) but if you do not, you may want to wear a mask.

A LAVENDER GARLAND

Dried lavender holds its scent for a long time—most other decorative dried plant material has no scent of its own at all. When making a garland from your own lavender, you can use it when it is fresh and then leave it to dry in the garland shape.

There are several ways of using lavender to make a garland. Tiny circlets can be made with small rings of stiff wire and a few flowering stalks—their charm lies in being small and simple. For larger and more elaborate garlands, you can still use wire, although crumpled chicken wire makes a firmer foundation.

Choose between different sorts of lavender foliage for an out-of-season garland, or use a mixture of foliage and flowering heads. For a well-perfumed and elegant garland, use bunches of flower heads from long-stemmed lavender with its foliage. The stems must be freshly cut with the buds not yet open; dried ones would be too stiff.

If you do not want the stems to show, cut off the flower heads, leaving short stalks, and push them into a ring of florist's foam. Arrange them so they all point in the same direction, lying close to the surface of the foam. You can use dried flower heads, but take care not to dislodge the buds. If you use fresh ones, leave the garland on a flat surface until the heads have stiffened; you will need lots of flower heads for this. To make a garland you will need florists' wire, a wire base, stout wire and a generous supply of freshly-cut lavender and/ or foliage.

1 Wire the lavender stems to an inner wire circle. Always use long stems with long flower heads as they will be easier to work with.

2 Work your way round the circle. The flower heads will splay out all round the ring. Distribute them as evenly as possible.

3 Wrap the stems, or bunches of stems, over the frame, then bring them under and inwards one at a time (or one bunch at a time).

4 Continue wrapping and weaving round the circle, fastening the flower heads unobtrusively with florists' wire.

BASKETS OF LAVENDER

*A*s holly is to Christmas, so lavender is to summer. In places where Christmas arrives in summer, lavender can be combined with more traditional greenery and can be used fresh or dried to create different effects, for swags, bunches, garlands and baskets. The stems can be interwoven with ribbon or tied into bundles ready to scent a fire, and the flower heads can be used as they are, or stripped, to make a satisfyingly fragrant filling for all sorts of containers.

Hybrid lavenders often grow into very large bushes with long straight stems. These are strong and pliable, and when made into bunches can be woven in and out of the uprights while baskets are made. The flower heads are left on and positioned inside the baskets, so they will always smell of lavender. It's easy to copy this idea with a ready-made basket (preferably an old one) that has widely-spaced uprights. Cut and pull out whatever has been woven between the verticals and replace it by weaving in bunches of fresh lavender. Keep the flower heads and stalk ends on the inside of the basket. It won't look very neat—that is part of its appeal—but it will release its fragrance as it dries out slowly.

If you have to cut off a lot of flower heads to make a pot-pourri, don't waste the stalks. They are scented too, although less so than the flowers, and can be burnt like incense sticks. If you have lots of stalks, a child may enjoy the methodical task of cutting them into lengths of between 2–4 in (5–10 cm) and tying them into neat bundles.

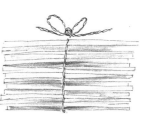

Use lavender bundles to scent the embers of a fire or put them on the hot metal surface of a woodburning stove to release their fragrance slowly. Be careful they do not catch fire.

To emphasize the regularity of lavender flowers, you can cram them into a straight-sided basket. To do this, place a block of floral foam in the basket and then cram in as many stems of lavender as you can manage.

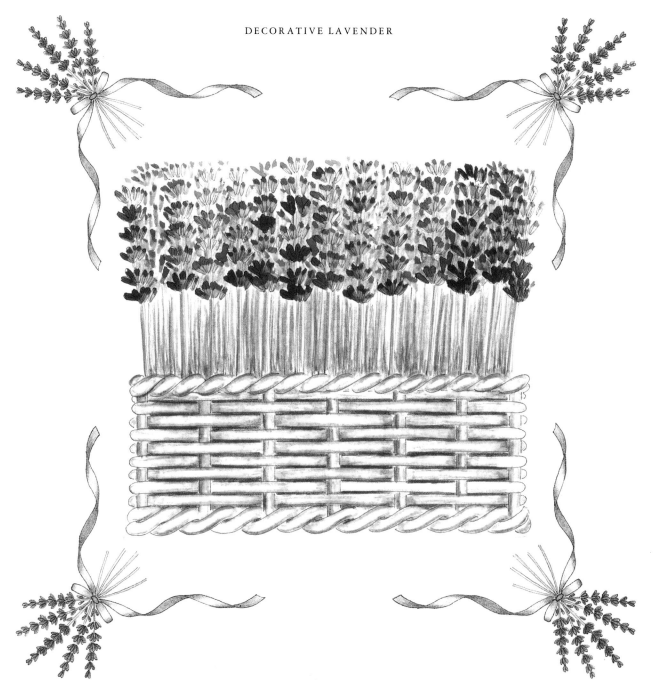

BUNCHES OF LAVENDER

Try to use complementary materials to tie up your lavender bunches. Jute string, cotton tape and old-fashioned rayon ribbon all look good, as do raffia and thick embroidery threads. However, nylon velvet ribbon can spoil lavender's simplicity.

When bunched and hung up to dry, lavender looks lovely and smells of summer. People who grow and dry their own lavender know that there are never enough places in which to hang the bunches for drying, unless they are lucky enough to possess a large airy barn. The bunches look so pretty that it seems a shame to take them down even when they are dry. In her book *Bella Vista*, Colette remarks on 'The smell of lavender, dried bunches of which were hung on the bedrail and in the cupboard', and anyone who owns a brass or iron bedstead could use lavender bunches to scent the bedroom.

Just as flowering stalks of lavender bushes can be anything up to 3 feet (90 cm) long, so bunches of lavender can be large sheaves, tiny posies or anything between the two. Try tucking little sprigs behind picture frames, or decorate mirror frames with larger, drooping bunches that hang down either side. You could fix armfuls of long-stemmed lavender along the top of an old cupboard or hang a big bouquet on a pine door. Tie small bundles to furniture or suspend from the ends of curtain poles.

One of the best, and also one of the simplest, ways of using dried lavender is to half-fill a beautiful shallow bowl with lavender flowers. Leave it near the telephone for playing with during calls—it is guaranteed to soothe frayed nerves!

Dried lavender is more robust than many dried flowers; it doesn't have the annoying tendency of some blooms to reabsorb moisture and turn floppy, and the stems are strong. Hybrid lavenders are more ready to let their flowers fall than species plants, so handle them with extra care. The pink- and white-flowered lavenders look rather dull when dried, and darker-coloured flowers generally give better results.

MAKING A LAVENDER BOTTLE

Making lavender bottles is an old pastime – they are fun to make and a pretty way to preserve lavender flowers in a cage of their own stalks. Any sort of lavender is suitable, but long stems will produce a different effect from short slender ones, so do experiment.

Because the effect of these little bottle-shaped baskets relies very much on neatness and regularity, it's essential to be methodical when making them. You'll need a surprising amount of ribbon, but it's quite hard to work out in advance how much. Two yards (two metres) is a good average. If you use narrow ribbon, such as ⅛ in (3 mm) wide, you'll need more; if you use wide ribbon, such as ¼ in (6 mm) wide, you will need less.

The number of stalks to be used must be worked out before you begin, otherwise the weaving will not come out right. Because you are weaving in a circular pattern, passing the ribbon over and under alternate stalks of lavender, you must start with an odd number of stalks. However, if your lavender has thin stems you may want to group them in twos or threes. In that case you may end up with an even number of stalks, but remember that the number of groups of stalks, like the number of single stems, must nevertheless be an odd one.

Lavender flower heads are fatter than the stalks so you may need to include some stalks with their heads cut off to make an adequate basket to contain the flowers.

After you have looked at the step-by-step instructions on page 45, you may like to try adapting them slightly.

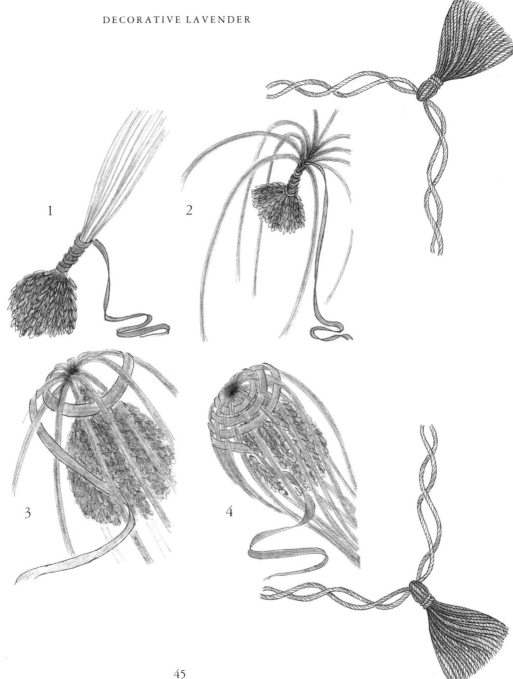

1 Bind stems
tightly
behind
flower
heads.

2 Bend
stems
back.

3 Grasp
bunch of
stems and
begin to
weave.

4 Weave
over and
under, round
and round,
arranging
stems evenly.

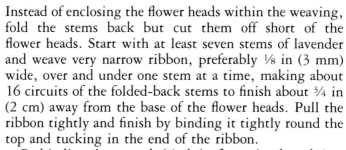

Instead of enclosing the flower heads within the weaving, fold the stems back but cut them off short of the flower heads. Start with at least seven stems of lavender and weave very narrow ribbon, preferably ⅛ in (3 mm) wide, over and under one stem at a time, making about 16 circuits of the folded-back stems to finish about ¾ in (2 cm) away from the base of the flower heads. Pull the ribbon tightly and finish by binding it tightly round the top and tucking in the end of the ribbon.

By binding the stems behind the flower heads and then folding the stems back on themselves you can make an unusual buttonhole posy. If you hang the finished boutonnière upside down to dry it will not wilt. *Lavandula stoechas* or *L. pedunculata* look particularly effective, since their colour bracts will retain their colour if dried carefully. Tiny lavender bottles make unusual and effective tree decorations at Christmas time. Use ⅛ in (3 mm) wide ribbon to weave over and under one stem at a time, starting with about 15 stems of lavender. Push the weaving down as you go and bind the top really tightly (the stems will shrink as they dry).

Larger bottles are too appealing to hide away in drawers and closets. Use ¼ in (6 mm) wide ribbon and weave it between sets of two stems at a time. To make a splendidly decorative object, loop tassels through the ribbon binding. Make two tassels and a length of twisted cord from embroidery thread and attach them to the top of the bottle. You can leave a lavender bottle on the bedside

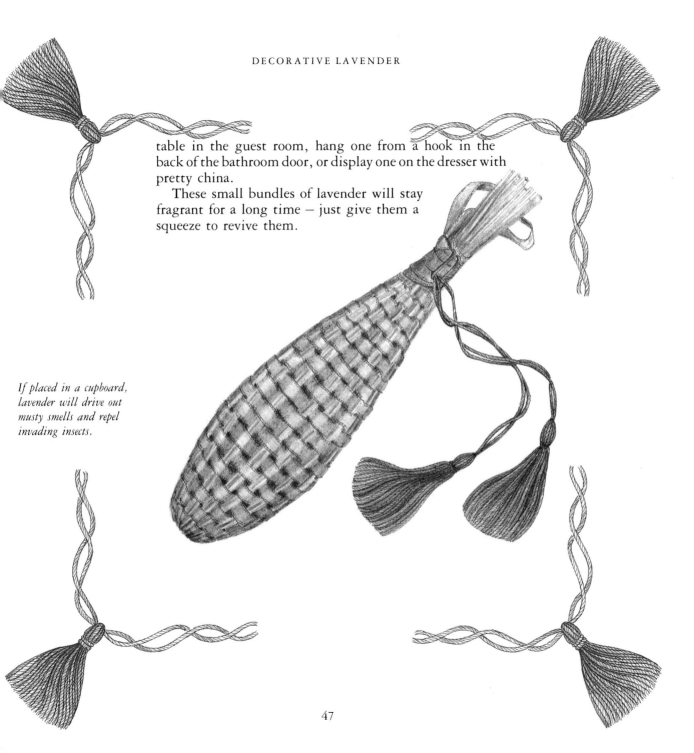

table in the guest room, hang one from a hook in the back of the bathroom door, or display one on the dresser with pretty china.

These small bundles of lavender will stay fragrant for a long time – just give them a squeeze to revive them.

If placed in a cupboard, lavender will drive out musty smells and repel invading insects.

ORNAMENTAL LAVENDER TREE

*B*efore you begin, consider the style of tree you wish to make. Would you like a rustic bush in a terracotta pot or a more elegant tree in a metal or china urn? You will need a container, a long stick or branch for the trunk, some general-purpose domestic filler, a ball of florists' foam and plenty of dried lavender spikes.

The trunk of the tree could be a gnarled and knobbly stick, a rough branch, or smooth dowelling which can be painted or bound with ribbon—do this in advance. When measuring the length of the trunk, add the depth of the container and half the depth of the foam ball to the visible length of the trunk. The size of the foam ball is up to you, but as a general rule it should be about twice the width of the mouth of the container.

Choose your container carefully. The tree's trunk will be fixed inside it with filler, so line the container with a double layer of baking foil if you wish to reclaim it later. However, if the pot is narrower at the top, you won't be able to remove the filler so use modelling clay instead.

Make a hole halfway into the foam ball, ready to receive the trunk, but don't push it in yet. Half-fill the container with a very stiff mixture of the filler and push the trunk firmly into it until it will go no further. Check that it is completely vertical. Now add a very little water to the filler to make it less stiff but not sloppy. Put a little into the hole you have made in the foam ball and push in the trunk, wiping away any excess filler. Leave overnight to set hard. Now follow the steps on the facing page.

Cut off a few lavender heads at a time, leaving stalks about 1 in (2.5 cm) long.

Starting from the middle of the foam ball, push in a vertical ring of closely-spaced flower spikes, then make other rings to the left and right. Always aim for the centre of the ball. The flower heads should be packed in tightly and evenly.

Fill up any gaps and then fill the container almost to the brim with pretty pebbles or dried lavender flowers. These little trees make good table centres or decorations for dressers and mantelshelves.

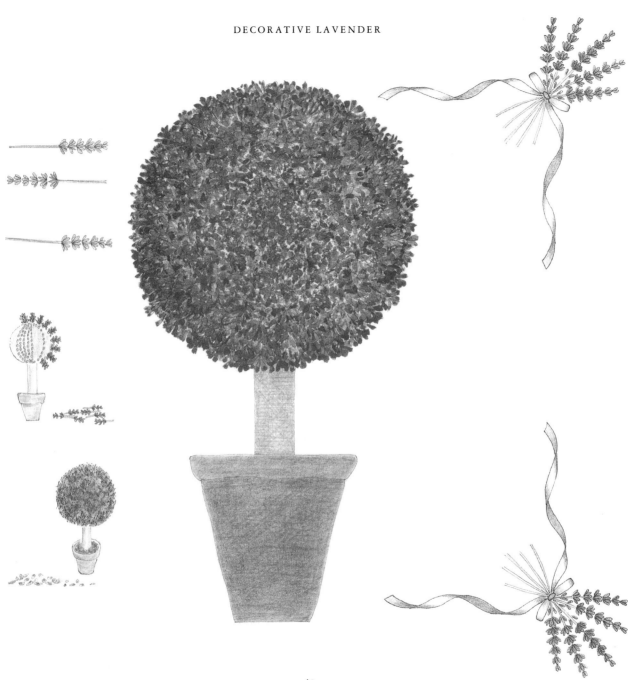

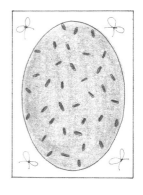

LAVENDER GIFTS

*L*avender is a must for people who enjoy making gifts for friends or for charity bazaars. An attractively tied bunch of lavender flowers makes a cheering keepsake, and simple sachets of dried lavender are easily assembled from scraps of fine fabric. Mrs Gaskell, in her novel *Cranford*, talks of 'Little bunches of lavender flowers sent to strew the drawers of some town dweller, or to burn in the room of some invalid.' Stems of aromatic plants were once burnt in sickrooms to disinfect and sweeten the air.

Because it is oily and not juicy, pressing lavender is simplicity itself. Place the stalks on a sheet of blotting paper laid on a flat surface, cover with another sheet of paper and pile several heavy books on top—then leave for several weeks. When you finally uncover them, the flowers will be ready to use on greetings cards, calendars or even framed decorations. You could create a little bush, a posy, or a basket of flowers.

For the basket, glue parallel lines of lavender stalks on to some paper to make the basket's uprights, then stitch horizontal lines of weaving through the backing paper with thick embroidery thread, over and under the uprights. Glue on the vertical lavender flowers so they touch each other. For the oval of dried flower grains, pencil in the layout first, then stick on each calyx (fresh or dried) with a tiny dab of glue. Press with books as above. All pressed flower pictures look best if pressed again after gluing but before adding the exterior mount. These cards also smell good when their envelopes are opened.

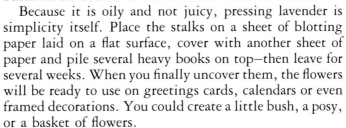

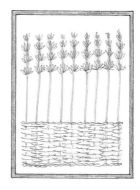

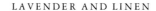

To make a lavender bag: first trace off
the design, then position it on the right
side of one of two rectangles (each about 6
x 4 in or 15 x 10 cm) cut from fine linen
or cotton, and transfer the motif.
Embroider the design with careful regard
to tension, using DMC stranded cotton
(floss). The buds are worked in detached
chain stitch in 333, the stems in stem
stitch in 523, and the bow in chain stitch
in 208.

Work with an embroidery frame to keep
the fabric taut and press from behind after
completing the embroidery. Hem the tops
of both the rectangles and with right sides
together stitch the other three sides together
to form a bag. Run gathering stitches
around neck, 1 in (2.5 cm) from the top.
Turn the bag right side out and fill with
lavender, then tighten the gathers, fasten
the thread and finish with a ribbon bow.

LAVENDER AND LINEN

MAKING A LAVENDER BAG

*L*avender has always been used for washing clothes (and people), so it should come as no surprise to learn that the words 'lavender' and 'launder' have the same Latin root. The connection is clearest in countries with Latin-based languages: the Spanish and Italian words for lavender, and the Latin word for laundry, are the same— *lavanda*. The French word, *lavande*, is said to be derived from the fourteenth-century Italian meaning of *lavanda*— that which is used for washing.

Lavender has a long-standing affinity with natural fabrics, and anyone who enjoys embroidery will find lavender indispensable. Some lavender species are particularly suitable for use inside sachets and pillows because of their very long-lasting aromas. With dried lavender flowers inside a sachet or pillow, it is natural to decorate the outside with a lavender motif.

Simple colour changes can be effective: for example, pale pink or white buds would work well on a pastel background. For best results, work on natural fabrics because synthetics tend to crinkle.

Lavender has an enduring fragrance, especially when protected from light, so do not discard lavender bags if their scent seems to have faded – squeezing the dried lavender will release more oils.

MAKING A SCENTED PILLOW

This design will suit a luxurious sachet or pillow. Enlarge the design to suit your pillow pad, but use the motif on the left (see facing page) as it gives the accurate position of the stitches. Cut out two pieces of your chosen fabric with a seam allowance of ⅜ in (10 mm) and transfer the enlarged design on to one of them.

Work all the flower heads in detached chain stitch, using two strands (three for a medium pillow and four for a large one). Work the stems in stem stitch with the same number of strands. The ribbon on the front of the pillow is not real but embroidered in long darning stitches. Work around the design once, then place each subsequent row of stitches alongside the first one to give the impression of satin stitches.

Make a frill from a long strip of fabric about 2½ in (6.5 cm) wide (increase it for larger pillows). Hem one edge and pull out threads about ⅜ in (10 mm) from that edge to take a ribbon ⅛ in (3 mm) wide. Thread the ribbon through in regular overs and unders, tie in a bow in one corner, and secure it with a stitch. Run a double row of gathers around the other edge of the frill and pin it in position, right sides together, round the embroidered front of the pillow case. Stitch all round, then pin the back of the case in position and sew around three sides. Turn it right sides out, and insert the pillow and a flat muslin pad filled with lavender flowers between the pillow and the cover. Oversew the fourth side.

Use the following DMC stranded cotton (floss) colours:

Flower heads: 333
Stems: 503
Ribbon: 210

EMBROIDERED WALL POCKET

*T*his embroidered fabric wall pocket is ideal for displaying dried lavender. Make a paper pattern to the correct size (see facing page), then cut out two triangles of interfacing. Place them glue side down on the wrong side of the fabric, so line A–B is parallel is with the selvedges. Allow an extra ⅜ in (10 mm) around each triangle, then iron on the interfacing and cut out the fabric triangles with their seam allowances. On the outer piece embroider a random pattern of detached stitches, representing lavender buds, in the four colours. Fold these edges over the interfacing on both pieces and tack (baste) them in place. Using long stitches, machine about 1/6 in (4 mm) from the edge around both pieces. Remove the tacking (basting) stitches. With a single strand of perle cotton, blanket stitch around the edges of both pieces, working into the holes left by the machine stitching. Carefully cut out and remove the machine stitching. Now work stem stitch along the bottom of the blanket stitch with perlé cotton to create a ladder effect—this is the ribbon casing. Following the manufacturer's instructions, use the fusing web, trimmed to fit, to bond the wrong sides of the triangles together. Make two eyelet holes where shown and use two strands of stranded cotton (floss) to work buttonhole stitch around them.

Oversew into the top of the blanket stitching on both sides all round the pocket with cotton perlé, then press the triangle over a thick pad of sheeting. While it is still warm, mould it into a cone and stitch the two short sides

MATERIALS
¼ yard (25 cm) medium-weight plain-woven lavender or mauve cotton fabric
¼ yard (25 cm) medium- or heavy-weight iron-on non-woven interfacing
Fusing web 10 x 10 in (25 x 25 cm)
DMC stranded cotton (floss) in dark lavender (333), pale lavender (340), pink (605) and white
Stranded cotton (floss) to match the fabric
Perlé cotton to match the fabric
Medium-sized crewel needle
1 yard (1 metre) of ⅛-in (3-mm) wide satin ribbon to match one of the embroidery colours

SIZE
The finished wall pocket is about 8 in (20 cm) deep

together. Thread the ribbon through the casing at the top of the cone and tie in a bow in the middle.

Hang up the wall pocket by inserting drawing pins (thumb tacks) through the two eyelet holes, then fill it with dried lavender and push dried lavender flowers into it.

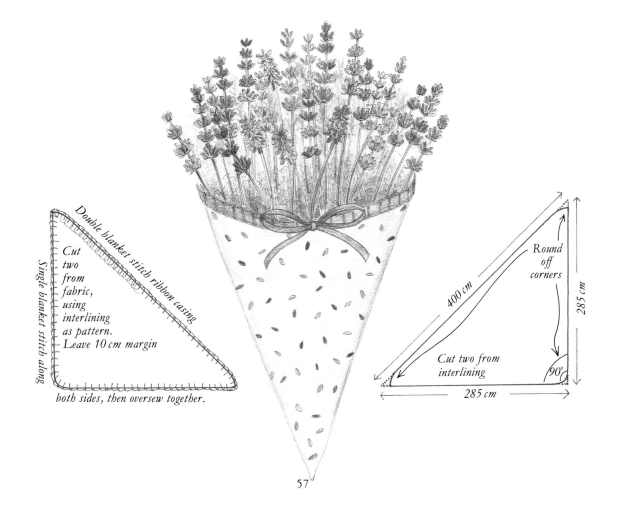

Single blanket stitch along

Double blanket stitch ribbon casing

Cut two from fabric, using interlining as pattern. Leave 10 cm margin

both sides, then oversew together.

400 cm

Round off corners

285 cm

Cut two from interlining

90°

285 cm

LAVENDER BLOUSE AND MAT

An embroidered spray of lavender makes a striking decoration for a crisp revers or a shawl-collared blouse, while a smaller posy looks pretty on a pocket. A bowl of lavender pot-pourri will be even more of a decorative feature if it is sitting on a matching mat embroidered with a sprinkling of lavender buds.

Transfer your chosen design from the facing page carefully on to greaseproof or tissue paper with an embroiderers' transfer pencil. If you want matching embroidery on either side of a collar you must reverse one of the designs. Work the sprays in two strands of DMC stranded cotton (floss), the flower heads in detached chain stitch and the stems in stem stitch. You can use the same colours as those on page 54 or any others you prefer— remember lavender can be white, pink or mauve as well as blue. White stitches on pastel fabric look especially pretty. The ribbons are worked in split stitch or stem stitch using one strand of DMC stranded cotton (floss) in a toning colour.

The mat is made from two thicknesses of linen with a layer of interlining sandwiched between them, so it will give some protection to a polished surface. The edge is worked with buttonhole stitch using one strand of DMC stranded cotton (floss) and the scattered lavender buds are worked with a mixture of colours (333, 340, 605, 327, 208) or just one of them. The two concentric circles are worked in chain stitch, using the same thread as that chosen for the buttonhole border.

Lavender has long been relied upon to scent linen and keep moths at bay; spike lavender (L. latifolia) or hybrids (lavandin) are best for this as they contain the most camphor. In the laundry, lavender was used for washing and rinsing. A lavender bush is the traditional place to spread out linen so that it can dry in the sun and take up the scent of lavender at the same time. Nowadays, lavender is widely used to perfume detergents and fabric softeners.

SCENTING LINEN WITH LAVENDER

*T*here are numerous ways to capture and retain the intoxicating summer fragrance of lavender, from the essential oil, lavender water and lavender-scented toiletries to lavender sachets and pillows. Padded clothes hangers stuffed with dried lavender will give you scented shoulders when you wear the clothes. The smell of lavender is never overpowering—it is an ingredient of many different perfumes because of its ability to blend with other scents, so it will not fight with any other fragrance you may choose to wear.

You can buy lavender-scented drawer liners or have the satisfaction of making your own. Simply choose a sheet of pretty wrapping paper, cut it to the size of the drawer and spread a layer of glue over the back. Cover thickly with dried lavender flowers, press down firmly until the glue dries and then shake the excess flowers on to a sheet of newspaper. Smooth the paper down into the bottom of a drawer, paper side up—the aromatic oils will give your clothes a wonderfully fresh smell. Rub your hand over the paper every now and then to release more oils.

The ladies of Victorian England used lavender in as many forms as they could. Muffs (or handwarmers) sometimes had dried lavender mixed with their stuffings and blocks of compressed flowers were carried in handbags or purses. Needlewomen used lavender in their own accessories such as pin cushions or needlecases; the oil in the dried flowers prevented the needles and pins going rusty. Small soft toys were sometimes partly stuffed with lavender to scent them.

The lavender bundles illustrated on page 45 were traditionally used as markers in the family linen chest or bride's trousseau, to indicate a dozen pillowcases, a dozen pairs of sheets, and so on. Today, you could use them when storing away clothes, blankets or any other items of linen.

LAVENDER DOLLY

*U*ntil the beginning of the Second World War, Germany exported dolls of all shapes and sizes to the UK. Miniature porcelain dolls often only had heads, arms and torsos, which could be no more than stuffed pads. Needlewomen would create the illusion of legs, concealed inside full skirts which took the form of tea cosies, powder puffs or, in this case, lavender bags.

You may be lucky enough to find one of these dolls in an antique market—they were made by the thousand and are still quite common, because they were exported to many countries.

Alternatively, you could improvise, as you really only need a simple wooden head with a neck and chest attached. The arms could be made from fabric or wood. Choose a pretty, soft, fabric for the skirt, then make it in the same way as the lavender bag (see page 52), but gather the top (this will be attached to the doll's torso). Turn it right sides out, stuff it with lavender and then gather it on to the doll's body, stitching it in place. This novel form of lavender bag makes an ideal present.

THE ESSENTIAL OIL

THE SCENT OF LAVENDER

*A*romatic plants are fragrant because they contain essential oils, in any or all of their parts—leaves, flowers, fruit or the rind of the fruit, seeds, stems, roots or bark. In the case of lavender, the oils permeate the whole of whichever plants are aromatic (a few species have hardly any smell at all). Many of the plants belonging to the labiat family, including lavender, live in hot dry places and have evolved ways of protecting themselves against dehydration. Essential oils help to reduce moisture loss and keep the plant cool.

The lavender species exploited commercially for their essences are *Lavandula latifolia* (spike oil) and *L. angustifolia* (true lavender oil), and the hybrid *L.* x *intermedia* (lavandin). The oil is concentrated in the calyx of each flower, which protects the emerging flower bud and, later, the developing seed. It is rare for plants with aromatic foliage to have plentiful oils in the flowers—it may be a device to ensure pollination and thus the survival of the species, because where lavender thrives so do ants. Like many other insects, ants dislike lavender oil and will go out of their way to avoid it (try using spike oil as an ant deterrent in the home or garden). Ants love sweet things, and if they were not repelled by the oil they might carry off the nectar without pollinating the plant. Instead, the nectar is left for the bees, who carry out their highly efficient job of pollination undisturbed.

HARVESTING

The oil produced by wild lavenders is much sought after by aromatherapists but it would not generally be economic today to exploit it on a commercial scale, although that is how the distilling industries in France and Spain began. Farmers and their families used small sickles to cut lavender and then took it down the mountains to be processed. At first they simply took whatever lavender they could find, but then their attempts to improve their yields by nurturing the wild plants led to the establishment of plantations in more accessible areas. Initially the bushes were planted singly in a grid pattern but eventually that too became uneconomic, and the plants had to be set out closely, in rows of hedges, so that they could be harvested mechanically.

DISTILLING LAVENDER OILS

*A*n eleventh-century Persian doctor, known in the West as Avicenna, is generally believed to have invented distillation. When he made his first distillate, attar of roses, alchemists were obsessed with the search for a way to transform base metals into gold, and it may have been those experiments that formed the basis of Avicenna's discovery. That is sheer conjecture, but it is true that distilling has a touch of alchemist's magic about it.

THE DISTILLATION PROCESS

A mass of plant material, in this case lavender, is packed into a large covered vessel (the still) which has a projecting pipe leading to another container (the condenser), inside which is a spiral tube surrounded by circulating cold water. Steam is introduced into the still, and as it passes through the flowers the heat of the steam makes the oil vaporize. The mixture of oil vapour and steam then passes into the condenser, where it is cooled back to a clear, pale gold liquid. The whole process lasts about one hour, although many people feel the best oil comes off in the first forty minutes. It takes roughly a quarter of a ton (tonne) of lavender to produce approximately 2¼ lb (1 kg/2¼ lb) of lavender oil.

Oils from *Lavandula angustifolia* (true lavender oil) or *L. latifolia* (spike oil) have been used for centuries, but up to and including the Middle Ages the species most used for distilling in southern France and Spain was *L. stoechas*. In the old days, all the oils distilled from

Before essences can be used they have to be separated from the plant material which contains them. For lavender, the process takes place in a still, or alembic, where steam passes through the plant material. The volatile oils vaporize, then are condensed and collected. In early pot stills the lavender was immersed in water which was then boiled over an open fire. An improved version had a grid on which the lavender was heaped, keeping it above the water level and thus raising the quality of the oil. Today, most distilleries use more sophisticated equipment for steam distilling.

any type of lavender were known as *Oleum spicae*, a name which occurs in fourteenth-century medical books. The third sort of oil, from *L.* x *intermedia*, or lavandin, is the newest commercial oil.

THE GROWTH OF THE LAVENDER INDUSTRY

Distilling lavender as an industry has progressed at different rates in different countries. In those where lavenders grow wild (such as France and Spain), the problems of collecting plant material from inaccessible

areas and transporting it to the distillery for processing meant the trade remained a cottage industry. Where lavender grew only as a cultivated plant (as in England), harvesting was easier because the distillery and plantation occupied the same site from the start.

In England, Potter and Moore's distillery was built in 1749 in Mitcham, on the outskirts of London, and was successful for almost two hundred years. Others soon followed, and gradually the industry spread far and wide over Britain, although it was generally in decline by the 1930s. According to one French grower, the time to plant lavender is when other growers are uprooting their bushes, so the timing was right when Norfolk Lavender, Britain's largest lavender farm, planted their first field in 1932 and began to distill their own lavender in 1936. At about that time in France, lavender distilling was changing from a cottage industry to a commercial undertaking, although that didn't happen in Spain until the late 1970s.

THE DISTILLERY

Distilling equipment has come a long way from the early days of primitive stills. Stainless steel has replaced copper for all new stills because it is much cheaper and easier to work. However, expert perfumers say that, for some reason, lavender distilled in copper stills produces a noticeably different oil from that distilled in stainless steel. All three of Norfolk Lavender's stills are made of copper, and two of them have been used for distilling lavender oil since 1874.

At the turn of the century, peasant farmers in France took their lavender harvests to itinerant distillers who carted their stills around the regions and then sold the oil to larger concerns, mainly for use in the perfumery industry. Later, the stills were given more permanent homes, near water, but irked by the difficult journeys and by loss of profit, prospering growers began to install their own equipment instead.

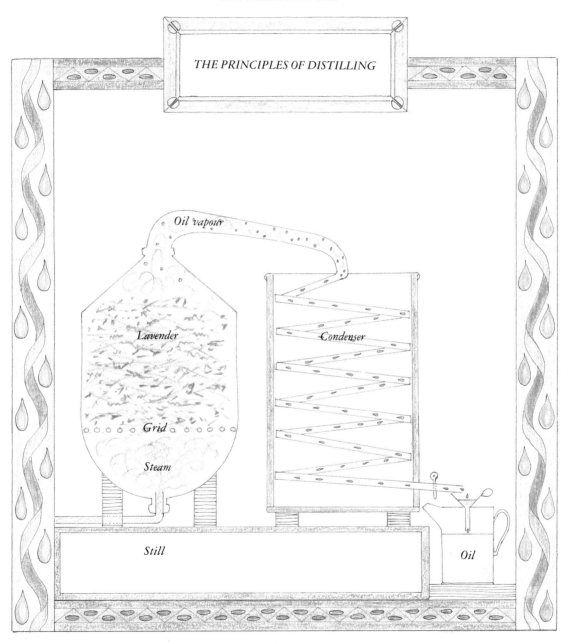

THE PRINCIPLES OF DISTILLING

Oil vapour

Lavender

Condenser

Grid

Steam

Still

Oil

LAVENDER IN PERFUMERY

*F*rance and England have become so widely associated with lavender that it's easy to forget these aren't the only countries where lavender is, or was, grown for distilling. Today, the industry also thrives in Australia, Spain, Italy, China, Japan, the USA, the USSR, Yugoslavia, Hungary, Algeria, Bulgaria, Romania (at least, until the 1989 revolution), Tasmania and Turkey. In fact, France is no longer the main supplier of lavender oil.

EAU-DE-COLOGNE—BY IMPERIAL APPOINTMENT

Germany has always been important in the perfume industry, and it is there that eau-de-Cologne was invented. Cologne is often thought of as an alternative name for eau-de-toilette, the dilute form in which many perfumes are sold, but actually they are not the same at all. Proper eau-de-Cologne is not just a perfume but a blend, with alcohol, of aromatic oils known for their stimulating properties. Bergamot oil is the principal ingredient, although lavender oil also plays an important role. While splashing it on, the wearer also inhales the scent and benefits from the oils, so it is a form of instant aromatherapy without the massage. It is deemed to be good for the morale, the health and for hygiene generally, as Napoleon Bonaparte must have found on his military campaigns—he used hundreds of bottles each year.

Eau-de-Cologne, or *Kölnisch wasser* as it was known first, was formulated in the early eighteenth century by Paul Feminis, an Italian living in Cologne (Köln) in

Germany. He passed the recipe to his great-grandson who in turn handed it down to his grandson, Johann-Maria Farina. Johann-Maria was a good salesman and gave both himself and his product French names, because apparently that was the way to sell perfumes. His was the original cologne ('This admirable preparation, known as eau-de-Cologne') favoured by Napoleon, to whom Farina was appointed purveyor by imperial appointment. The same formula is still available today, under the Gallicized name of Jean-Marie Farina.

THE VERSATILITY OF LAVENDER

The use of lavender oil in eau-de-Cologne is a good example of one of its virtues in perfumery: it blends well with other oils and enhances their qualities. Colognes are dominated by citrus scents—one recipe for 'Superfine eau-de-Cologne' lists oils of balm, citron, lemon, petitgrain, neroli, limetta, bergamot and Portugal sweet orange oil (all of which are redolent of citrus), as well as lavender and rosemary.

Lavender is a component (often unnoticed) of a large number of fragrances designed for men, who might turn up their noses at its supposedly feminine connotations if they knew it was there. Lavender's ability to combine with other oils and release their powers has made it the most useful and versatile oil in aromatherapy. In its own right it has so many therapeutic uses that, of all the aromatic oils, it is truly the essential one. It is of low toxicity and can be used undiluted in an emergency, for small burns and cuts as well as for insect bites.

LAVENDER WATER

*E*au-de-Cologne was one of the first distilled toilet preparations to use oils in combination. Most other scents were single-note floral fragrances until synthetic blended perfumes arrived on the scene. Of all the floral scents, rose, violet and lavender were probably the most popular, and lavender was always a particular favourite because of its extra tonic and cosmetic properties.

ADVERTISING STRATEGIES

For over two hundred years lavender water was the principal product of numerous distillers, and there was plenty of competition between them. Manufacturers' claims ranged from the wonderful powers of their product and no one else's, to claims (true or otherwise) to be the largest, oldest-established or sole purveyor of the only genuine article. Lavender water was presented in a gloriously varied range of bottles, from elegantly tasselled decanters to garish or amusing novelty phials. Often the

Lavender water was often sprinkled so a special bottle cap was fitted as standard for many years. This silver-coloured cap sat in a cork, thus providing a narrow spout, and had its own tiny screw cap. For more generous applications the whole device, including the cork, could be pulled out.

An elegant continental refinement offered a cap which unscrewed to reveal two small slots in the top, but which could not be completely removed and lost.

Some bottles designed for carrying around were especially appealing. A popular design had a brass lid with a long silk or rayon tassel. The bottle had a pointed base to make it obvious that it was not meant to stand up but was intended to be tucked into a bag or pocket.

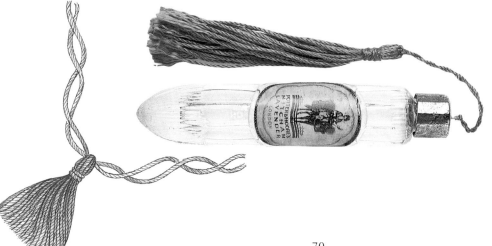

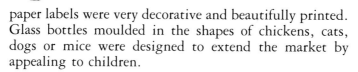

paper labels were very decorative and beautifully printed. Glass bottles moulded in the shapes of chickens, cats, dogs or mice were designed to extend the market by appealing to children.

A 'GREEN' FRAGRANCE

A standard recipe for lavender water would have contained 4 fl oz (120 ml/4 fl oz) of lavender oil, 6 drops of tincture of musk, 4 gallons (15 litres/4 gallons) of perfumers' spirit and ½ gallon (1.9 litres/½ gallon) of distilled water. This basic formula was often made more exotic by adding ambergris, more musk, vanilla, tuberose, violet, tolu balm or rosewater. Today, lavender water is usually made without such animal products as ambergris and musk, and without the need for animal testing.

Sixteenth-century Europe saw a craze for home distilling, and all sorts of concoctions, decoctions and infusions were made on a domestic scale. There was a pervading interest in all things floral (much as there is now), and every housewife wanted a still of her own. It is tempting to copy this historic pursuit but there are drawbacks. It takes a great deal of lavender to make even one drop of oil, and the necessary distilling equipment is hard to come by. Perfumers' spirit, which is used for making lavender water, can also be difficult to obtain (unless you hold the appropriate licences) and is very expensive. Infusion is the answer—you can steep successive batches of lavender flowers in a relatively scentless oil or spirit at home (almond or refined olive oil, vodka or gin are all ideal), but don't expect to save any money by doing so!

In the past, serious users of lavender water regarded it as an indispensable part of their daily toilet and so bought it in large bottles. Washing facilities were not always as widespread as they are now, and the alcohol in lavender water meant it evaporated quickly and therefore could be used for various cleansing purposes.

As well as restoring the senses, smelling salts were also something pleasant to sniff at a time when the world was a very smelly place, in the days of horse-drawn transport. They also acted as instant air purifiers for the fastidious, because they contained germicidal ingredients.

LAVENDER FOR LADIES

*A*s well as being a main ingredient of perfumes and toilet waters, lavender was widely used in the manufacture of smelling salts, which were for so long an indispensable requisite for any lady worthy of the name. Midway between a perfume and a medicament, they were used to ward off, or aid recovery from, the frequent fainting fits caused mainly by tightly laced corsets. The smelling salts were often packed in bottles very similar to the circular ones used for portable lavender water, and were a continuation of that earlier aromatic accessory, the vinaigrette.

French bottles of smelling salts were much closer to vinaigrettes because, like them, they were generally much prettier and more ornate than English ones. French women recovered from their swoons with the help of acetic acid fumes (as in vinegar), whereas it was ammonia that made Englishwomen's eyes water. Whatever the reviving medium, the aromatic oils in the mixture were used for their germicidal qualities as well as their scent, and were credited with health-giving benefits for the throat and respiratory system. Even when the salts were perfumed with another flower essence and labelled, for example, as wallflower or rose geranium salts, the mixture would nearly always include some lavender oil for its fortifying effects.

When fainting went out of fashion so did smelling salts, and lavender distillers had to start thinking of new guises in which to market their wares. The stock items

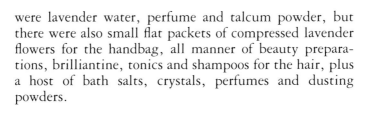

were lavender water, perfume and talcum powder, but there were also small flat packets of compressed lavender flowers for the handbag, all manner of beauty preparations, brilliantine, tonics and shampoos for the hair, plus a host of bath salts, crystals, perfumes and dusting powders.

OILS OF SPIKE AND LAVANDIN

Traditionally, all sorts of detergents, shampoos, soaps, liquid cleaners and other household items have been scented with spike lavender. Spike oil gives a clean, fresh smell to a multitude of cleaning products; yet, remarkably, spike lavender has never really been cultivated in the same way as true lavender. Even in the late 1970s cultivation had only just begun to take over from the wild harvest, and when that happened it was usually lavandin which was planted.

Spike oil is now uncommon, but if spike lavender had not hybridized with true lavender, there would have been no lavandin. Lavandin oil has been a godsend to distillers worldwide because, although it is not of such good quality as oil from *Lavandula angustifolia,* it is better than spike and perfectly adequate for perfuming soaps, cosmetics and detergents.

Perfumers and aromatherapists use oil from *L. angustifolia* in high class products, and in England the oil produced from Norfolk Lavender's fields all comes from varieties of *L. angustifolia.*

Spike oil has always been seen as inferior to true lavender oil and was used to eke out and dilute the more expensive oil because, although cheap, its quality was reliable. In the cheapest products it replaced lavender oil completely. This is well illustrated by comparing several traditional recipes for soap. The best quality soaps (eau-de-Cologne, millefleur, marshmallow and patchouli, as well as lavender), contain a good proportion of lavender oil. However, as the soap gets cheaper the amount of lavender oil is reduced until, in economy versions, it is replaced completely by spike oil.

OILS IN MEDICINE

Oil from *L. angustifolia* has long been catalogued in Pharmacopoeia (the official dispensing lists for pharmacists) under the Latin name *Oleum lavandulae {flores}*. Its medicinal status has been reinforced by other epithets, including *officinalis, vera* and *legitima*, which distinguish it from the impostor, spike oil.

Ironically, the only way that spike lavender would have appeared on the label of a chemist's jar was in the form of the varnish on the label, of which it was a component! One of the unfavourable qualities often attributed to spike oil is that it is high in camphor.

Despite being generally scorned as a medicinal oil, a small bottle of spike oil is very useful as a general aid to health. A few drops sprinkled on a handkerchief will clear a blocked nose, and one drop on a sugar lump or mixed with a spoonful of honey will ease a sore throat.

AROMATHERAPY

The word 'aromatherapy' was first used by the Frenchman René-Maurice Gattefossé, and his book of that same name, first published in 1928, is one of the standard early works on the subject. His experimental use of lavender oil when treating burns is well known in the world of aromatherapy, and he showed just how effective lavender oil can be.

The treatment of a wide variety of conditions, both internal and external, by massage with aromatic oils is readily accepted in France but is perhaps regarded as rather a novelty in the UK. In hotter countries, where the healing herbs grow wild, there is a tradition of herbal medicine which, although reduced by the introduction of more modern drugs, remains unbroken, and lavender has an important part to play in it.

BUYING LAVENDER OIL

True lavender oil has always been subject to adulteration, and this can be hard to detect. Lavender oil is a very precious commodity and therefore is very likely to be diluted in some way, so take great care that you buy the very best quality, especially when paying the sums commanded by good oil. Buy only from suppliers who have a good name to protect, and even then always ask about the origin of the oil. Be suspicious of any supplier who can't, or won't, answer any questions. The best course, whenever possible, is to buy directly, or by mail order, from the distiller. An anonymous bottle simply

Lavandin plants may yield as much as ten times more oil than comparable lavender plants and are more amenable to organized cultivation. Their flowers are easier to harvest mechanically because they are all roughly uniform and because they bloom all at once instead of over several weeks.

labelled 'lavender oil' may contain true lavender oil, but it may also contain spike oil or blended lavender oils. Even if it does contain true lavender oil, this may have been eked out by adding cheaper oils—something that should be reflected in the lower price. If you want to economize you will get a better bargain by mixing the oils yourself.

You will probably also get better value for money if you buy your own bath or massage oil base, and add to it as much or as little pure lavender oil as you wish. Lavender oil keeps well if stored in a cool dark place and, except when kept in a tiny bottle for travelling purposes, it is best consigned to a blue or brown glass bottle, with a dropper for accurate dispensing.

Supply and demand fluctuate, and a labour-intensive product can become uneconomic before being raised to the status of a luxury item. Ironically, that is what has happened to the original true lavender oil from the French Alps, which is now setting the standard for the high-quality oils used in aromatherapy.

USING LAVENDER OIL IN AROMATHERAPY

Like all essential oils, lavender should only be administered under qualified supervision, and it must always be kept away from the eyes. However, its undoubtedly beneficial effects can be enjoyed at home when it is diluted for bathing and massage.

Lavender oil will repel insects if rubbed into exposed parts of the skin. Spike oil has always been the best choice because it contains more camphor, which insects hate, and it is cheaper than other lavender oils. True lavender oil can be used to treat acne, eczema, dermatitis and other skin problems (but only under medical supervision). Its anti-fungal qualities make it an effective and fragrant way to control athlete's foot. A small bottle of true lavender oil is a good addition to a first aid box and is particularly useful on a journey.

A FINAL BOUQUET

Lavender-scented products and perfumes were a feature of so many areas of daily life for so long that lavender acquired an old-fashioned image. Just when the lavender market was failing and labour problems were causing added economic difficulties, new outlets for lavender began to appear in the manufacture of detergents and a variety of cosmetic products which were unknown at the beginning of the twentieth century.

Rationalization has led to more efficient and profitable ways of cultivating and processing lavender, and the rebirth of aromatherapy has led to new uses for the oil and a heightened awareness of all lavender's potential benefits. There is also a resurgence of interest in such traditional pastimes as drying flowers and making pot-pourri. Today, gardens and gardening are enjoying a steady increase in popularity, and the search for interesting and worthwhile plants has led to the reappearance of several lavenders loved in the Middle Ages or Victorian era. Lavender, the plant with a past, is also the plant for the future.

BIBLIOGRAPHY

Detailed and accurate information about lavenders is worth seeking out in libraries, particularly those of horticultural and botanical institutions. Old gardening books and herbals often include references to lavenders.

The first comprehensive survey of lavender was made by Miss D. A. Chaytor in her monograph *A Taxonomic Study of the Genus Lavandula*, published in the Journal of the Linnean Society Volume 51 pp. 153–204 (1937–8). Additional botanical information is given by Anthony G. Miller in *The Genus Lavandula in Arabia and Tropical N.E. Africa* [Notes of the Royal Botanic Gardens Edinburgh Volume 42 (3) pp. 503–528 (1985)], and by Arthur O. Tucker and Karel J.W. Hensen in *The Cultivars of Lavender and Lavandin* [Baileya, Volume 22 (4) pp. 168–177 (1985)].

First published in 1826, *The Natural History of the Lavenders* by Baron Frederic de Gingins-Lassaraz is still useful and interesting. In 1967 it was translated from the original French by members of the New England unit of The Herb Society of America (300 Massachussetts Avenue Boston Mass. 02115). Only 500 copies were published so, again, a library is the answer.

Lavandes et Lavandins by Christiane Meunier, published by Édisud (ISBN 2–85744–216–5 1985) deals with the history of lavender cultivation in France. *The Story of Lavender* by Sally Festing, published by Heritage in Sutton Leisure (ISBN 0–907335–18–7 1989), tells of lavender growing in England.

For information about the uses of lavender in the perfume industry and in aromatherapy, two helpful books are *Perfumes, Cosmetics and Soap*, by W.A. Poucher (ISBN 041–21066–04) and *The Art of Aromatherapy* by Robert Tisserand (ISBN 0–85207–140–X).

INDEX

aromatheraphy, 69, 76–7, 78
Avicenna, 64

bags, lavender, 53
baskets, 40, 51
bees, 12, 62
blouses, embroidered, 58
bottles, 44–47, 69, 70–2, 73
bunches, 43

camphor, 58, 75, 77
cards, 51
Colette, 43
Cologne, 68–9
colours, 32
cooking, 13–21
cotton lavender, 27
crystallized flowers, 14–15
cultivation, 30
cuttings, 34

Dioscorides, 8–9
distilling oils, 64–7, 72
dolls, 61
drawer liners, 60
drying lavender, 36–7
'Dutch' lavender, 26

eau-de-Cologne, 68–9, 70
embroidery, 53–8
England, 24, 66, 68
essential oils, 62–7

Farina, Johann-Maria, 69
Feminis, Paul, 68–9
foliage, garlands, 38

France, 26–7, 63, 65–6, 68, 76, 77

garlands, 38
Gaskell, Mrs, 51
Gattefossé, René-Maurice, 76
Germany, 68–9
gifts, 51–61
greeting cards, 51
ground cover, 35
growing lavender, 30

harvesting, 36, 63, 65–6
hedges, 34–5
honey, 12
hybrids, 12, 28, 30

ice, lavender yoghurt, 17
infusions, 72
insect repellant, 77

lavandin, 12, 26, 28, 30, 34, 37, 58, 62, 65, 74
Lavandula x *allardii*, 25, 26
Lavandula x *angustifolia*, 10, 12, 14, 22, 26, 27, 28, 30, 32, 34, 35, 37, 62, 64, 74, 75
Lavandula canariensis, 10, 28
Lavandula delphinensis, 30
Lavandula dentata, 10, 22, 25, 28, 34, 35
Lavandula dentata candicans, 22, 35
Lavandula 'Hidcote', 34
Lavandula x *intermedia*, 26, 27, 28, 32, 34, 37, 62, 64, 65

Lavandula lanata, 10, 22, 34, 35
Lavandula latifolia, 10, 12, 14, 25, 27, 28–30, 35, 58, 62
Lavandula multifida, 9, 10, 22. 28, 34
Lavandula pedunculata, 28, 35
Lavandula pinnata, 10, 28, 34
Lavandula spica, 26, 27, 28
Lavandula stoechas, 9–10, 28, 32, 34–5, 64
Lavandula viridis, 10, 28, 32, 35
lavender water, 25, 69, 70–2
Limonium sinuatum, 27
linen, scenting, 60–1
Linnaeus, 27, 28
liqueurs, 20–1

marmalade, 16
mats, embroidered, 58
medicine, 75, 76, 78
meringues, 19
Mitcham, 24–6, 66,
moths, 58

Napoleon Bonaparte, 68, 69
Norfolk Lavender, 2, 25, 66, 74

oil, 7, 12, 62–7, 74–5, 76–8
'Old English lavender', 24, 25, 26
Oleum spicae, 65

perfumery, 68–75
pillows, scented, 54

pink lavenders, 32
polishes, 12
pot-pourri, 36
Potter and Moore, 24, 66
pressing lavender, 51
propagation, 34

recipes, 13–21

Sackville-West, Vita, 37
salads, 15
Santolina chamaecyparissus, 27, 35
scented pillows, 54
scents, 60–1, 68–75
sea lavender, 27
seeds, 34
smelling salts, 72, 73
soap, 75
soils, 30
Spain, 63, 65–6, 68
spike oil, 12, 28, 62, 64, 74–5, 77–8
standard plants, 35
stems, 40
sugar, 20, 21
syrups, 20, 21

tea, lavender, 21
trees, ornamental lavender, 48

wall pocket, embroidered, 56
white lavenders, 32

Yardley's, 25
yoghurt ice, lavender, 17

CREDITS

Lois Vickers would like to thank David and Elizabeth Christie of Jersey Lavender for their generous help, and staff at the Lindley Library and the Linnean Society Library for help with research. Thanks are also due to Ruth Warner for access to The Ruth Warner Collection of perfume bottles and for permission to reproduce items on page 11 (lower) and page 74, and to Robert Opie for permission to reproduce the labels on pages 75 and 76. The engraving on page 65 is reproduced by kind permission of The Mary Evans Picture Library. Other photographs by Jon Stewart.